The
Adventures
of
Lil' Jack Jack

Michelle G.

To order additional copies of this book, contact:
Xlibris
844-714-8691
www.Xlibris.com
Orders@Xlibris.com

ISBN: Softcover   978-1-6698-7518-5
               EBook   978-1-6698-7517-8

Print information available on the last page

Rev. date: 04/22/2023

The **Adventures** of **Lil' Jack Jack**

It was another warm, sunny day at Pleasant View Farm. The meadow, as always was lush and green; butterflies danced by the brightly colorful flowers that trimmed the walkway and birds sang songs. Signifying that spring was well underway.

Old man Willard was going about his usual, early morning chores. There he sits, propped on his tiny stool, nestled by good ole' Daisy, milking away. *"It's going to be a great day today Daisy...I just know it!"*

Patches, the honorary feline of Pleasant View Farm, is still beaming over her five little bundles of joy that she welcomed a couple of months ago. 'Izzy' short for Isabell, Tucker, Cali, Scout and Lil' Jack Jack. Izzy is a spitting image of her mother Patches; and quite rambunctious. Tucker is a momma's boy, that never strays too far from Patches. Cali is far more reserved and, sometimes she just doesn't know what to make of Izzy. Scout is a true leader of the pack, always letting his voice be heard. And Lil' Jack Jack, smallest of the litter, always the observant one and has a curious nature about him; that can sometimes get him into trouble.

It's now feeding time and Lil' Jack Jack is having difficulties making his way through his bigger brothers and sisters. He pushes and prods to no avail and finally decides to wait until their through. Old man Willard is making a racket in the cow barn with Daisy, so while everyone is busy filling their bellies, Lil' Jack Jack ventures off to find out what all the commotion is about. He enters the cow barn and finds a bucket of milk, has spilled all over the floor. So, he does what any good feline would; he makes a valiant attempt to lap it all up. You can always count on Lil' Jack Jack to help a friend in need. To his surprise and delight, old man Willard turns to find Lil' Jack Jack lapping up the remaining drops of milk. *"Where did you come from little one?"* Old man Willard said with a curious pause.

Lil' Jack Jack draws his gaze up, licking his lips, gives old man Willard a sweet meow. "Meow". Old man Willard smiles, shakes his head and wipes his brow. He scoops up Lil' Jack Jack and says, *"Come on now...we'll have to get you back to your mama...a little one like you shouldn't be out here wandering around by yourself"*. Old man Willard strolls over to find Patches with her four little babies nestled in a pile of hay. As Patches awakens, old man Willard places Lil' Jack Jack beside her. *"Looks like this one got away from ya!"* Old man Willard chuckled..." *better keep a close eye on that one."* Patches gave her little Jack a few licks and then fell fast asleep.

Morning came and everyone on the farm was still overjoyed about the new babies…well everyone except for Konnie Kluck. Konnie Kluck is well known on the farm; many will say that she isn't pleasant at all. Konnie has always been known to be unpredictable, and downright territorial, so staying away from her pen is an absolute must! That afternoon the five siblings played and played until the sun went down. After they filled their bellies, they all settled in for the night…well except for Lil' Jack Jack. Lil Jack was still pondering about the delicious milk he had savored the night before, so he decided to venture out to see if old man Willard had left some behind. What's the worst that could happen?

Fearful of the dark, he sprinted as fast as he could over to the barn door and just as he was about to peek inside, Konnie Kluck shoved her big beak out from behind the door. *"KLUCK KLUCK!"* she shrieked. Terrified of her massive body and huge beak, Lil' Jack Jack darted, but it wasn't easy to hide from the seasoned Konnie, she knew the farm all too well. Lil' Jack Jack ran, jumped and leaped through the raspberry bushes as fast as he could, ultimately ditching the wicked Konnie Kluck but there was one problem…he didn't know where he was. Jack looked around hoping to see his mother or siblings but found nothing. He knew the raspberry bushes would provide a safe place for the night, so he tucked himself in and fell fast asleep.

Before too long, morning arrived, and Jack awoke to the warmth of the sunshine and two big eyes staring right at him. A bit scared at first, Jack let out a big meow, attempting to sound tough, *"MEOW!"* but his new large friend wasn't fazed at all. In return, he let out a loud *"NEIGHHHHH!"* This big fella's name is Prance. Prance is one of the friendliest and most energic horses on the farm. He welcomes anyone and everyone that stops by his stable. Prance has a very regal way about him too. When excited he will trot, kick and prance around...hence the name, Prance. *"Hi, I'm Prance!"* he said, with delight. *"Hello, my name is Lil' Jack Jack. I've seemed to have lost my way; can you point me in the direction of the farm?"* Prance was making such a commotion over the new visitor that it drew the attention of Prance's best friend Ginger.

Ginger is a sweet ole' gal that finds Prance's enthusiasm delightful. Ginger is a true beauty, with a long ginger mane and an even longer ginger tail. Lil Jack Jack showed his appreciation for all their attention by purring and rubbing back and forth on the raspberry bush. *"I wonder what my family is doing right now."* Jack thought to himself with a bit of concern. Jack let out a final meow to the horses to bid them a fine farewell then headed on down the road. Jack followed the raspberry bushes one by one hoping to finally see his mama and siblings.

He came across a beautiful monarch butterfly, with bright orange colors and deep black outlines around the edges of its wings. Lil' Jack Jack was curious and wanted to introduce himself to the beautiful butterfly. But every time he got close, his new friend would just flutter away to an adjacent flower. This went on and on for some time, as Jack moved further and further away from his family. The butterfly guided Lil' Jack Jack across a large open field brimming with beautiful colorful flowers and a small wood line that didn't seem too far across. Lil Jack Jack saw the sunshine and wanted to see what was on the other side. As he trotted over the hill, he could see a massive house off in the distance and wondered *"I wonder who lives there?"*

As he approached the house, he heard a soft humming sound coming from the front yard. He crept through the boxwoods and peeked through the daylilies to find a lady tending to her flowers. She is tiny in stature with dark brown hair and big brown eyes. Her overall demeanor seemed peaceful and sweet, something Lil' Jack Jack found irresistible. Jack Jack was so excited to finally see someone that he leaped out of the bushes and let out a loud *"MEOW!"* Michelle was startled at first but that quickly changed when she laid eyes on Lil' Jack Jack. *"Hello, there little one!"* Michelle said cheerfully. *"Where did you come from?"*

Lil' Jack Jack immediately threw himself on the ground and rolled back and forth with excitement. Michelle then crouched down next to Lil' Jack, smiled and rubbed his belly. *"I've never seen you around here before… you must be hungry".* Lil' Jack Jack looked up with his big green eyes and let out an even louder *"Meow! Meow!".* *"Ok ok",* Michelle giggled, *"I'll get you something right away, I hope you like chicken?"* Michelle quickly headed inside to fill two bowls, one with shredded chicken and another bowl with fresh water. She quickly gathered up both bowls and headed to the door. When she opened the door, she found her new little friend waiting patiently. *"You're such a handsome little boy…I hope you're hungry!"* Michelle placed the two bowls on the front porch and watched Lil' Jack Jack devour every morsel.

"Whoa! That didn't take long." She giggled again. After finishing his meal, Lil' Jack Jack wasted no time jumping onto Michelle's lap to show his appreciation for her gracious hospitality. Michelle sat for some time enjoying her new friend's company and promised Lil' Jack Jack that she would help him with not only food for his belly but help him find his family. *"Someone must be worry sick about you." I know I would be if you were wondering out here all by yourself." "Don't worry, tomorrow, I will post some flyers but for now, you'll be safe here with me."* The days came and went, and no one ever responded to the flyers. No phone calls…no emails…no one. Yet every day Michelle would open her front door to find Lil' Jack Jack waiting patiently for her.

"Morning little one!" Michelle said happily. *"I have some breakfast for ya."* She gave Lil' Jack a big smile as he purred and walked back and forth bumping her leg. And again, she sat and watched Lil' Jack clean his plate of food never leaving a bit behind and always returning to her lap to thank her for the food given. *"Ya know something little one…it might be a good idea for you to call this your home. I know you'd like it here… what do you think?"* Michelle stood up and placed Lil' Jack Jack down on the front porch. Lil' Jack looked saddened at first because they usually spend more time together however this time when Michelle opened the front door, she invited him in. *"Come on little one!" "Come inside with me!"* She said, cheerfully. Lil' Jack Jack wasted no time on this invitation and immediately ran inside the house.

Once inside he gazed upon a large room filled with new toys and a new bed. *"See!"* Michelle said with excitement. *"You have toys to play with and a soft warm bed!"* *"I'm quite certain you'll find it softer and warmer than the mulch chips outside."* Michelle giggled. She then walked over to her favorite oversized chair by the windows. *"Come with me."* She motioned with her hand. Lil' Jack Jack quickly followed. *"This is where I spend most of my time."* She sat down on the chair with the warm rays of sunshine shining on her back. Lil' Jack Jack jumped onto the chair with such enthusiasm and came nose to nose with Michelle. *"Ha! Ha! You always make me laugh little one."* *"What should we name you?"* Michelle pondered while looking at her new little friend with the big green eyes. *"I know!"* Michelle said with delight. *"I'll name you after my late grandfather, Jack."* *"How's that sound?"* Michelle asked. Lil Jack Jack looked at her with amazement and let out his loudest meow yet. *"MEOW!"* *"Well then, it's settled. We'll call you Jack...Little Jack."*

As Little Jack purred and curled up on Michelle's chest, she wrapped her arms around him and whispered, *"Welcome home Little Jack."* At that moment, Little Jack realized that he was never lost, he had been heading in the right direction all along.

Meet the Author Michelle and Lil' Jack Jack

This book is dedicated to my beloved father.

As you watch over us,
may I continue to make you proud.

Printed in the United States
by Baker & Taylor Publisher Services